Bats in my attic
READER KLEINHENZ

Bats
in My
Attic

Written by Sydnie Meltzer Kleinhenz
Illustrated by Rick Stromoski

Children's Press®
A Division of Scholastic Inc.
New York • Toronto • London • Auckland • Sydney
Mexico City • New Delhi • Hong Kong
Danbury, Connecticut

**To my Valley Oaks kindergarten students of 2003-2004.
You're all in my Happy Book.**
— S.M.K.

For Molly
— R.S.

Consultant
Eileen Robinson
Reading Specialist

Library of Congress Cataloging-in-Publication Data

Meltzer Kleinhenz, Sydnie.
  Bats in my attic / written by Sydnie Meltzer Kleinhenz ;
illustrated by Rick Stromoski.
    p. cm. — (A Rookie reader)
  Summary: When a group of friends gather to play baseball in the backyard,
they go to the attic to get the bats and find they are black, furry, and alive.
  ISBN 0-516-24865-0 (lib. bdg.)   0-516-25022-1 (pbk.)
  [1. Baseball bats—Fiction. 2. Bats—Fiction.]
I. Stromoski, Rick, ill. II. Title. III. Series.
  PZ7.M5165Bat 2005
  [E]—dc22
                              2004030080

I think weekends are for baseball.

3

Everybody is playing tonight.
Rosemary has bases.

Tim and Jim have baseballs.

I have bats in my attic.

"Come on, Mom. Tonight we play baseball and it's almost dark," I say. "Do you have everything?" Mom asks.

"Where are the bats?" Rosemary asks.

"The bats are in my attic. Can you get them?" I ask.

Rosemary runs out of the house.
"There are bats in the attic!" she yells.

"Why are you so upset?" Jim asks.
"I'll get the bats."

Jim runs out of the house.
"There ARE bats in the attic," he says.

"Yes, I know," I say.
"Tim, can you please get them?"

Tim runs out of the house.
"There are BATS in the attic!" Tim says.

Yes. Bats are in my attic.
They are in my toy box.

Word List (70 Words)
(Words in **bold** are compound words.)

a	dark	I	playing	think
almost	do	I'll	please	Tim
and	**everybody**	in	**Rosemary**	to
are	**everything**	is	runs	tonight
ask	fly	it's	say	toy
asks	for	Jim	says	upset
attic	get	know	she	we
baseball	gets	Mom	**shortstop**	**weekends**
baseballs	**grandmother**	**mothball**	so	where
bases	has	my	that's	why
bats	have	of	the	yells
box	he	out	them	yes
can	high	**outfield**	there	you
come on	house	play	they	

About the Author

Sydnie Meltzer Kleinhenz teaches fourth grade in Houston, Texas. She lives with a dog, a one-legged parakeet, and numerous reptiles, amphibians, and fish. She also has five loveable sons. Her published credits include many poems, magazine articles, and over 50 books on the shelves of both stores and schools.

About the Illustrator

Rick Stromoski is an award-winning humorous illustrator and syndicated cartoonist. His favorite animals are bats.